Happy Holidays!

Valentine's Day

by Rebecca Sabelko

BELLWETHER MEDIA
MINNEAPOLIS, MN

Blastoff! Beginners are developed by literacy experts and educators to meet the needs of early readers. These engaging informational texts support young children as they begin reading about their world. Through simple language and high frequency words paired with crisp, colorful photos, Blastoff! Beginners launch young readers into the universe of independent reading.

Sight Words in This Book 🔍

a	get	on	the
and	go	out	they
day	he	people	to
eat	is	red	up
for	it	some	we

This edition first published in 2024 by Bellwether Media, Inc.

No part of this publication may be reproduced in whole or in part without written permission of the publisher. For information regarding permission, write to Bellwether Media, Inc., Attention: Permissions Department, 6012 Blue Circle Drive, Minnetonka, MN 55343.

Library of Congress Cataloging-in-Publication Data

LC record for Valentine's Day available at: https://lccn.loc.gov/2023001669

Text copyright © 2024 by Bellwether Media, Inc. BLASTOFF! BEGINNERS and associated logos are trademarks and/or registered trademarks of Bellwether Media, Inc.

Editor: Christina Leaf   Designer: Laura Sowers

Printed in the United States of America, North Mankato, MN.

Table of Contents

It Is Valentine's Day!

We send cards and candy. It is Valentine's Day!

card

What Is Valentine's Day?

Valentine's Day
is on February 14.

The day honors **Saint** Valentine. He stood up for love.

Saint
Valentine

It is a day
to show love!

A Day for Love!

People give cards. They give flowers and candy.

candy
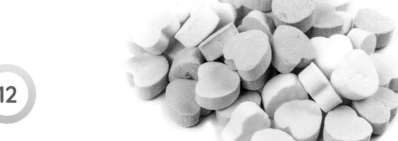

flowers

13

People wear
red and pink.
They put up hearts.

hearts

People dress up.
They go out
to eat.

Some people give rings. They get **engaged**!

ring

getting engaged

It is fun to show love on Valentine's Day!

Valentine's Day Facts

Celebrating Valentine's Day

card

Happy Valentine's Day!

candy

flowers

Valentine's Day Activities

give cards

wear red and pink

put up hearts

Glossary

engaged

promised to be married

saint

a special person in Christianity

To Learn More

ON THE WEB

FACTSURFER

Factsurfer.com gives you a safe, fun way to find more information.

1. Go to www.factsurfer.com.

2. Enter "Valentine's Day" into the search box and click 🔍.

3. Select your book cover to see a list of related content.

Index

The images in this book are reproduced through the courtesy of: Stephanie Frey, front cover; Sergiy Bykhunenko, p. 3; Michael Kraus, p. 4; yurakrasil, pp. 4-5; TierneyMJ, p. 6; lisegagne, pp. 6-7, 20-21; Zvonimir Atletic/ Alamy, pp. 8-9; Black-Photography, p. 10; Dollydoll29, pp. 10-11; Elizabeth A. Cummings, p. 12; CameraCraft, pp. 12-13; 1981 Rustic Studio kan, p. 14; Narongrit Sritana, pp. 14-15; Olena Yakobchuck, pp. 16-17; kritskaya, p. 18; Studio Romantic, pp. 18-19; Evgeny Karandaev, p. 22; kirin_photo, p. 22 (give cards); Pixel-Prose, p. 22 (wear pink or red); JasonDoiy, p. 22 (put up hearts); wavebreakmedia, p. 23 (engaged); www.brockbuilt.com/ Wikipedia, p. 23 (saint).